WORKBOOK FOR

THE ONE TRUTH

(A Guide to Jon Gordon's Book)

Your Powerful Guide on Elevating Your Mind, Unlocking Your Power and Healing Your Soul

ABOUT JON GORDON

American author and speaker Jon O. Gordon (born January 20, 1971) focuses on leadership, culture, sales, and cooperation.

The Los Angeles Dodgers, Pittsburgh Pirates, San Diego Padres, Miami Heat, Oklahoma City Thunder, University of Georgia Bulldogs, Clemson Tigers, University of Nebraska Athletic Department, Jacksonville Jaguars, Philadelphia Eagles, San Francisco 49ers, Atlanta Falcons, Campell Soup, Wells Fargo, Northwestern Mutual, Publix, Southwest Airlines, and the University of Georgia are just a few of the teams, universities, and businesses that Gordon has collaborated with. He has a lot of experience working with teachers and principals from kindergarten through high school in various North American educational systems.

Originally published in 2015, Gordon's "The Energy Bus Animated Training Program" is an interactive course based on Gordon's best-selling book The Energy Bus. Gordon established Positive University in 2016 as an ongoing online program with resources for coping with life's typical stresses and bringing like-minded people together.

Gordon's writing has been featured in numerous newspapers and magazines, including the aforementioned Washington Post, New York Post, Wall Street Journal, and U.S. News & World Report.

He graduated from Cornell with a degree in human ecology and from Emory with a master's degree in education.

Jon Gordon's motivational presentations and books have been seen and heard all around the world. Numerous Fortune 500 corporations, professional and collegiate sports teams, school systems, hospitals, and non-profits have all put his beliefs to the test.

He has written 28 books, including 14 New York Times bestsellers and five works for young readers. Among his works are the multi-million copy bestsellers The Energy Bus, as well as the award-winning The Carpenter, Training Camp, The Power of Positive Leadership, The Power of a Positive Team, The Coffee Bean, Stay Positive, The Garden, and the recently released The One Truth.

The Today Show, CNN, CNBC, the Golf Channel, Fox & Friends, and countless more news outlets have all highlighted Jon and his advice.

His list of clients reads like a who's who of American business: from the Los Angeles Dodgers to Campbell's Soup to Dell to Publix to Southwest Airlines to Snapchat to Truist Bank to Clemson Football to Northwestern Mutual to West Point Academy.

The Master of Arts in Teaching that Jon earned at Emory University complements his bachelor's degree from Cornell. His training and consulting firm has made it its mission to foster the growth of inspirational leaders, productive businesses, and cohesive groups.

**THIS ONE WEEK OUTLINE WAS
DEVELOPED TO HELP YOU.**

➤ The foremost thing
  is to find a
  person you can rely on to
  help you achieve your
  goals if you want to be
  successful.

➤ Be careful not
  to make any mistakes
  when filling out the vital
  forms displayed below.

➤ Consider each day's tip,
  task and prescription
  carefully.

**THINK ABOUT THEM
MEDITATIVELY.**

➢ **Everything you learned in the note should be written and meditated upon.**

Also, jot down your thoughts and feelings, as well as the obstacles you've come to terms with.

READ AND LISTEN TO
EVERYTHING
THAT IS BEING SAID
AND RECOMMENDED.

Without a doubt, adhere to
them.

IT WAS MADE TO BE
POSSIBLE.

Never doubt the fact that
you
can do it, and never give up
hope.

**YOU'RE ALL SET TO STEP
ON TO THE NEXT LEVEL!**

Ensure that you fill out the Form below in its entirety.

DATE IT ALL BEGINS

_____

_____

DATE OF FINAL CONCLUSION (Usually 7 D ays from the starting Date)

_____

Fill in the blanks with your name and email address:

_____

_____

FILL OUT YOUR AGE

_____

_____

**It's not as difficult as you might
think, but don't take it for
granted and keep going.**

**Recommendations and
Tasks for the Day Don't End
That Day; Carry On and
Make Habits of Them.**

DAY 1

INSIGHT

Study and practice how to pour out all your troubles and sorrow before almighty God, knowing that he is God and is capable of healing you of your grievances and pain.

WHAT YOU SHOULD IMBIBE TODAY

Pray fervently to God for anything it is that is stealing your peace. Ask him to come to your assistance and heal you of your troubles.

<u>DON'T FORGET...</u>

When you pray to God, remove doubt, understanding that you are talking to the Lord of host and King of Kings.

MEDITATE

_____

_____

_____

_____

_____

_____

_____

_____

_____

_____

_____

_____

_____

_____

_____

_____

_____

_____

_____

_____

_____

_____

_____

_____

_____

_____

_____

_____

_____

Don't doubt the power of the most High God, don't hide anything from him or feel your need is much.

DAY 2

INSIGHT

Accepting the things you can't change or control is one of the most effective ways of attaining peace and happiness in life.

WHAT YOU SHOULD IMBIBE TODAY...

Stop battling those things that are bigger and stronger than you, ignore them and build yourself. Doing this on its own makes you the boss over them.

DON'T FORGET...

You empower things by paying
attention to them!!!

MEDITATE

_____

_____

_____

_____

_____

_____

_____

_____

_____

_____

_____

_____

_____

_____

_____

_____

_____

_____

_____

_____

_____

_____

_____

_____

_____

_____

Ignore hate and losers, that's the much they can do with their miserable lives.

DAY 3

INSIGHT

Forgiving your offenders of the bad things they did against you has more positive impact in your life than you ever imagine. It gives you peace, happiness, mental clarity, grace and more.

WHAT YOU SHOULD IMBIBE TODAY

Reflect on all the people that have done you bad in the past, commit their evils into God's hands, forgive them, forget them and move on with your life and personal effort for growth and progress.

DON'T FORGET...

To err is human but to forgive is divine!!!!

MEDITATE...

_____

_____

_____

_____

_____

_____

_____

_____

_____

_____

_____

_____

_____

_____

_____

_____

_____

_____

_____

_____

_____

_____

_____

_____

_____

_____

_____

**Letting go of people's
offence opens greater
doors in your life.**

DAY 4

INSIGHT

Correct meditation takes you far away
from the thieves of your peace; it
opens your mind to correct decisions
that make your life better.

WHAT YOU SHOULD IMBIBE TODAY

In a quiet place, sit calmly and
meditate on life. Ponder on your
problems and how to solve them.

<u>DON'T FORGET…</u>

Proper meditation opens your mind up
to unseen reality and impending
dangers.

MEDITATE

_____

_____

_____

_____

_____

_____

_____

_____

_____

_____

_____

_____

_____

_____

_____

_____

_____

_____

_____

_____

_____

_____

_____

_____

_____

_____

**In every single day that passes,
think about your life!!!**

<u>DAY 5</u>

<u>INSIGHT</u>

Regardless of how busy you think you are in this world, making out time for yourself would always be more profitable. Find yourself and your peace in this chaotic world.

<u>WHAT YOU SHOULD IMBIBE TODAY...</u>

Force out time for yourself today. Sit back on your own and find the places you're lacking. Solve your problems from now.

<u>DON'T FORGET</u>

Even if you over stress and die, the
world will still move on!!!

MEDITATE

_____

_____

_____

_____

_____

_____

_____

_____

_____

_____

_____

_____

_____

_____

_____

_____

_____

_____

_____

_____

_____

_____

_____

_____

_____

_____

**Don't let the chase of
anybody drain you of your
energy, it's not worth it.**

DAY 6

INSIGHT

Visualize your dream life and happy place, knowing and believing that you'd reach there sooner than later.

WHAT YOU SHOULD IMBIBE TODAY

As you work hard, motivate yourself to keep moving by imagining your dream life. Imagine how it feels when you've finally hit your goals.

DON'T FORGET

Imagining your dream life, when channeled properly would aid you in reaching it sooner than you expect.

MEDITATE

_____
_____
_____
_____
_____
_____
_____
_____
_____
_____
_____
_____
_____
_____
_____

_____

_____

_____

_____

_____

_____

_____

_____

_____

_____

_____

Dream it until you make it!!!

DAY 7

INSIGHT

Having hope in God regardless of what life throws at you makes you invincible because you've now rooted yourself in him (God). Don't forget that he is the master planner, preparing something big for you.

WHAT YOU SHOULD IMBIBE TODAY

Build yourself to hope and trust in God regardless of how heavy the storms around you gets.

DON'T FORGET

God is the alpha and omega, he can always make a way even paces where there appears to be no way!!!

MEDITATE

_____

_____

_____

_____

_____

_____

_____

_____

_____

_____

_____

_____

_____

_____

_____

_____

_____

_____

_____

_____

_____

_____

_____

_____

_____

_____

_____

_____

_____

_____

**God is wisdom, when you
remember him, you should stop
doubting the process.**

YOU'VE FINISHED WITHTHIS ONE WEEK GUIDE. KEEP UP WITH IT.

POSITIVE RESULT COMES WITH IT.

Show Love to people by giving them copies of this.

_____

_____

_____

_____

_____

_____

_____

_____

_____

_____

_____

_____

_____

_____

_____

_____

_____

BYE!

Each time you're deviating, return to this!

Made in the USA
Monee, IL
10 January 2024

51500167R00026